Original title:
Stronger with Time

Copyright © 2024 Swan Charm
All rights reserved.

Author: Olivia Oja
ISBN HARDBACK: 978-9916-89-697-6
ISBN PAPERBACK: 978-9916-89-698-3
ISBN EBOOK: 978-9916-89-699-0

Guiding Stars of Resilience

In shadows deep, we seek the light,
The stars above shine ever bright.
With faith in hearts, we rise and stand,
Together we walk, hand in hand.

Through trials faced, our spirits soar,
Each challenge met, we learn to roar.
In grace we find our strength anew,
With love and hope, we journey through.

The path may twist, the way may bend,
Yet, steadfast love will never end.
With courage borne from heavens high,
We reach for dreams that touch the sky.

In prayerful whispers, wisdom flows,
The heart knows peace, the spirit grows.
With every step, we rise above,
In unity, we find true love.

The guiding stars, they shine so clear,
They lead us on, they calm our fear.
In every heart, a flame ignites,
A beacon bright in darkest nights.

The Wisdom of Years

In the stillness, whispers flow,
Ancient truths in hearts we sow.
Each year a gift, a lesson learned,
In patience shines the wisdom earned.

Guided paths of light divine,
In shadows deep the stars align.
Through trials faced, our spirits rise,
With every tear, the soul complies.

A gentle heart, long time embraced,
In quiet moments, grace is traced.
The hands of time, a tender guide,
In every heartbeat, love abides.

Transcendent Growth

From seed to tree, the journey spans,
In sacred soil, the purpose plans.
Each breath a step in sacred dance,
Awake the soul to chance romance.

Life's seasons turn, in sun and rain,
The spirit blooms through joy and pain.
In quietude, the mind expands,
With open heart, the world commands.

Each challenge met, a chance to rise,
In darkness found, the light that tries.
With faith as roots, we reach for skies,
In every fall, the strength implies.

Sacred Echoes Through Time

In silence echoes ancient song,
A melody of right and wrong.
Through ages past, the truths resound,
In every heart, the lost are found.

From prophets' lips to sages' hands,
The wisdom flows in shifting sands.
In every whisper of the breeze,
The sacred calls, the spirit frees.

Through shadows cast, the light will break,
In courage found, new paths we make.
With unity, compassion's glow,
The timeless love begins to grow.

Rays of Celestial Understanding

In dawn's embrace, the light appears,
A gift of hope that calms our fears.
With every ray, the soul expands,
In unity, divinity stands.

Through trials faced, the heart ignites,
In darkest nights, we seek the lights.
With open mind, the heavens call,
In small moments, we find it all.

Each lesson penned in starlit skies,
In faithful hearts, the truth replies.
Through every breath, we come to know,
In love we grow, in love, we glow.

Transcendent Roots

In the depths where silence dwells,
Our spirits weave through sacred spells.
Connected deep, in faith we rise,
Transcendent roots beneath the skies.

Through whispers soft, the truth unfolds,
In hearts of seekers, grace beholds.
In every breath, a purpose found,
In ancient wisdom, we are bound.

From earth to sky, our souls do soar,
In harmony, we seek the more.
With open hands, and hearts so pure,
Transcendence is the light, the cure.

Through trials faced, we learn to shine,
In darkness deep, our spirits twine.
With love as guide, our path is clear,
Transcendent roots in faith we steer.

Through the Veil of Ages

Through the veil of ages past,
We seek the truth that ever lasts.
In shadows deep, the light will creep,
Illuminating what we keep.

With every prayer, the echoes ring,
A gentle song our hearts do sing.
In time's embrace, we find our call,
The sacred dance of one and all.

From ancient scrolls to whispered dreams,
Through night's dark veil, the spirit gleams.
In unity, we rise as one,
Through shining stars, our journey's begun.

The tapestry of life we weave,
In love and grace, we truly believe.
Through every moment, hand in hand,
Together strong, together stand.

Grace in the Twilight

In twilight's glow, the world feels still,
The heart rejoices, and dreams fulfill.
In gentle hues, the spirit sighs,
A moment blessed, where grace complies.

Each fleeting breath, a sacred song,
In tranquil whispers, we belong.
With eyes uplifted, we see the way,
In God's embrace, we find our stay.

With every dusk, a promise made,
Through trials faced, we are not swayed.
In quiet grace, our fears dissolve,
With faith as light, our souls evolve.

In twilight's peace, we find our rest,
Through every shadow, love is blessed.
In every heart, a spark ignites,
Grace in the twilight, our guiding lights.

Embracing the Infinite

Embracing wide, the infinite flow,
In love's embrace, our spirits grow.
With every breath, a sacred bond,
In unity, our hearts respond.

With open arms, we greet the dawn,
In every moment, life goes on.
In harmony, we dance and sing,
Embracing all that grace can bring.

Through trials deep, we learn to trust,
In faith and hope, we find what's just.
With every heartbeat, joy ignites,
In paths of light, our future writes.

Together strong, we stand as one,
Embracing life, in truth begun.
In love's embrace, we rise and soar,
The infinite waits, forevermore.

Chosen by the Dawn

In the stillness, light unfolds,
A whisper beckons, stories told.
Hearts awaken, souls ignite,
Chosen by the dawn's soft light.

Mountains bow to morning's grace,
Every shadow finds its place.
Guided by the hopeful song,
In the dawn where we belong.

Birds take flight, their voices rise,
Melodies fill the painted skies.
Hope is born with every ray,
In the light, we find our way.

Hands united, faith in bloom,
Chasing dreams that cast away gloom.
Together, we shall walk this path,
In His love, we find His math.

Morning breaks, the world renews,
With every step, we seek His views.
Chosen by the dawn so bright,
In His arms, we find our light.

In the Shadow of Eternity

In the quiet of the night,
Stars whisper tales of sacred light.
In the shadow, peace does reign,
Embracing all with love's sweet strain.

Time stands still, a moment's grace,
Eternity's touch, a warm embrace.
Within the depths, our spirits soar,
In the shadows, we are more.

Hearts entwined in silent prayer,
Lost in dreams, yet always there.
A dance of hope, a life divine,
In the shadow, love will shine.

With every trial, we shall learn,
In the night, our candles burn.
Holding fast to faith's embrace,
In the shadow, find our grace.

Eternity calls through the dark,
Filling hearts with love's bright spark.
In the shadow, we take flight,
Bound in joy, we greet the light.

Revelations of Age

Time weaves tales on weathered skin,
In wisdom's glow, new life begins.
Every wrinkle, a story shared,
In revelations, none are spared.

Through the years, we learn to dance,
In the echoes of fate's chance.
Seasons change, yet still we stand,
Embracing all with open hand.

Lessons whispered in the breeze,
Songs of ages put us at ease.
In the garden of the past,
Revelations bloom, hold fast.

Faith grows deeper as we age,
Turning every leaf, a page.
With each heartbeat, grace bestowed,
In revelations, love's road showed.

As twilight falls, the fire's warm,
A gentle hush, a guiding charm.
Together, we shall traverse the stage,
In every dawn, our truth, our age.

Tides of Understanding

Waves of truth upon the shore,
Guiding hearts to seek and soar.
Tides of faith, they ebb and flow,
In their grace, we come to know.

Every ripple tells a tale,
In the storm, we shall prevail.
Through the depths, we find our way,
In the tides where hopes shall sway.

From the ocean, wisdom gleams,
In the currents, we find dreams.
Embracing change, we understand,
Together, we shall make our stand.

Salt and sand, the sacred blend,
In each wave, the soul transcends.
In the surf, where hearts align,
Tides of understanding, divine.

As the sun sets, prayers arise,
In the twilight, faith never dies.
With open hearts, we'll take the chance,
In the tides, we find our dance.

Resilience of Spirit

In shadows deep, our faith does gleam,
Strength renews like a flowing stream.
Through trials fierce, our hearts ignite,
With hope as our guide, we find the light.

With every storm, we rise anew,
A tapestry of grace, we weave it true.
For in the pain, there's beauty found,
In whispered prayers, our souls are bound.

From ashes rise, we claim our place,
In unity, we share His grace.
The chains of doubt, we cast away,
In love's embrace, we choose to stay.

Each tear we shed, a seed is sown,
In barren soil, we find our own.
With steadfast hearts, we walk the line,
In every struggle, His light will shine.

The Alchemy of Existence

From dust to stars, our journey flows,
In sacred bonds, our spirit grows.
Each moment a gift, each breath a theme,
In the grand design, we dare to dream.

With open hands and hearts laid bare,
We share our burdens, we lift in prayer.
Through every trial, gold we find,
In love's embrace, our souls aligned.

Transformation blooms in darkest nights,
Illumined paths, our spirits take flight.
In every loss, a lesson speaks,
In silent whispers, divinity seeks.

To live is to learn, to love is to heal,
In every hardship, our truth revealed.
With grateful hearts, we face the day,
In sacred journeys, we find our way.

Chiseling the Soul

As stone and hands, a sculptor divine,
Mold us to reflect the sacred line.
With every chisel, we shed the past,
In every stroke, our essence cast.

The dust of life, we carve with care,
Imperfect shapes laid bare, we share.
In patience found, our spirits grow,
In trials faced, our strength we show.

Each chip of doubt, a path reveals,
In faith and love, our truth unveils.
We strive for grace in every fold,
In every story, the heart is bold.

Through pain and love, resilience shines,
In the master's hands, our soul aligns.
With courage strong, we break the mold,
In unity, our hearts unfold.

Celestial Meditations

Beneath the stars, we find our peace,
In quiet nights, our worries cease.
With whispered prayers, we touch the sky,
In sacred moments, we learn to fly.

The moonlight bathes our souls in grace,
In stillness, we encounter His embrace.
With every heartbeat, the universe sings,
In heavenly tunes, our spirit clings.

Each breath a prayer, a moment divine,
In the vast expanse, our souls entwine.
In celestial realms, we seek the truth,
In the dance of life, we reignite youth.

The stars align, our paths unfold,
In quiet strength, our hearts behold.
With every thought, we reach above,
In celestial meditations, we find love.

Resilience in Sacred Shadows

In shadows deep, we find the light,
A whispering hope in the night.
Through trials forged, our spirits rise,
With faith as our guide, we touch the skies.

Beneath the weight, we stand our ground,
In sacred whispers, grace is found.
The storms may come, the winds may blow,
Yet in our hearts, love's embers glow.

Every tear, a lesson learned,
In every trial, our courage burned.
For in the dark, His wisdom stands,
A beacon bright, in our trembling hands.

With steadfast hearts, we journey on,
In sacred paths, we are not alone.
Through every shadow, light will stream,
In faith we walk, and in hope we dream.

Seasons of Grace

In springtime blooms, the heart takes flight,
With fragrant petals, the soul ignites.
Summer's warmth, a gentle embrace,
In every moment, we find His grace.

Autumn leaves, like blessings fall,
Each golden hue a sacred call.
In winter's chill, we learn to rest,
In quietude, we feel His best.

The cycle turns, and so we grow,
In every season, His love must show.
Through trials faced, and joys embraced,
In every breath, we feel His grace.

With open hearts, we welcome change,
In every curve, no need for strange.
For in His hands, we find our way,
In faith and love, we choose to stay.

The Unfolding Journey

With every step, the path is clear,
A call to wander, to hold what's dear.
In valleys low, our spirits soar,
For every moment, we seek what's more.

Mountains high and rivers wide,
In Nature's arms, we choose to bide.
Through winding roads, and skies of blue,
In every heartbeat, His love shines through.

The journey weaves, a tapestry,
With threads of faith, and harmony.
In every trial, a lesson to find,
In every challenge, our hearts aligned.

With open eyes, we greet the dawn,
In every challenge, we can't go wrong.
As we unfold, hand in divine hand,
Together in love, we take our stand.

Enduring Light

In darkest hours, You are our guide,
Through every shadow, You are beside.
Your light, a flame that never wanes,
In every sorrow, Your hope remains.

With steadfast hearts, we carry on,
In every struggle, Your strength is drawn.
Through trials faced, we rise anew,
For in Your love, our souls break through.

The path ahead may twist and turn,
Yet in Your embrace, our hearts do yearn.
In faith's bright light, we find our way,
With every dawn, we greet the day.

In silence deep, Your whispers call,
With open hearts, we surrender all.
As we walk forth, our spirits ignite,
In every moment, we find Your light.

Eternal Foundations

In shadows long and light so bright,
We build our dreams on faith's pure sight.
The stones of hope, they carry weight,
Through trials fierce, we find our fate.

United souls in sacred bond,
We rise together, ever fond.
The heart of love, our guiding star,
Leads us through paths both near and far.

With grace we stand, through storm and strife,
Embracing truth, we share this life.
In moments small, the spirit speaks,
In whispered prayers, the heart still seeks.

Beneath the heavens, stars align,
Our footsteps marked by love divine.
In every breath, a promise made,
Eternal light shall never fade.

So let us walk this sacred ground,
With open hearts, our purpose found.
In faith we trust, in hope we sing,
For in our hearts, His peace we bring.

The Ascending Path

With each ascent, our spirits soar,
The mountains high, the valleys poor.
In every step, His grace we feel,
The way ahead, a holy seal.

The winding road, though steep and long,
Is paved with faith, a sacred song.
Together we tread, with hearts aglow,
In search of truth, we strive to grow.

The trials faced, they mold our soul,
In every challenge, we become whole.
A light within, our constant guide,
Through darkest nights, He's by our side.

We find our strength in quiet grace,
As hand in hand, we seek His face.
Through every storm, we hold on tight,
For He is with us, our source of light.

On this path where angels tread,
With every step, our spirits fed.
In love's embrace, we rise anew,
With faith unwavering, pure, and true.

Faith Through the Ages

From ancient times, the stories flow,
Of those who walked and dared to know.
In pages worn and voices strong,
The echo of the faithful throng.

Through trials vast and shadows deep,
In every tear, our promises keep.
With courage bold, we face the night,
And walk together toward the light.

In whispers soft, the past does teach,
The hand of God, it's always reach.
Through every age, His love remains,
In joy and sorrow, in losses, gains.

With hearts aflame, we share the grace,
Transforming lives, we find our place.
In every moment, a sacred chance,
To dance in faith, in love's expanse.

For faith is more than words expressed,
It's living love, it's being blessed.
Through ages old, one truth we share:
In faith we stand, for God is there.

Whispers of the Divine

In quiet moments, hear His call,
The gentle voice, it beckons all.
Through rustling leaves and waters clear,
In nature's realm, our hearts draw near.

The morning dew, a sign of grace,
A tender touch, a warm embrace.
In every breeze, His love we find,
In sacred whispers, souls unwind.

In shadows cast by fading light,
We seek His presence in the night.
Each prayer we lift, a sacred lift,
A gift of love, our souls adrift.

In silence deep, we hear the hymn,
The heart's refrain, a sacred whim.
In every heartbeat, every sigh,
The whispers of the divine draw nigh.

So let us pause, and still our mind,
In every breath, His love defined.
For in the silence, truth is known,
In whispers soft, we are not alone.

The Passage Becomes You

In the stillness of dawn's embrace,
The soul begins its gentle flight,
Through the murmuring paths of grace,
Seeking the veil of sacred light.

With each step, the heart expands,
Touching realms both near and far,
In the echo of ancient bands,
Finding peace beneath the star.

The whispers guide along the way,
Leading through valleys deep in prayer,
Every moment a soft relay,
To awaken love and share.

Journey forth with faith's sweet song,
Knowing the passage holds the key,
To where the heart does truly belong,
In the arms of divinity.

Here, the passage is not lost,
But the essence of who you are,
Each footfall counts, no matter the cost,
For you are forever, a shining star.

The River of Becoming

Flowing gently, the river calls,
Carving paths through rock and sand,
Where the spirit dances and enthralls,
In the embrace of God's own hand.

Currents swift, yet soft, profound,
Over stones that gleam and shine,
In its depths, wisdom is found,
As the sacred waters entwine.

Surrender to the ebb and flow,
Trusting in the divine design,
With every ripple, the truth shall show,
That life's a journey, pure and fine.

As the river meets the sea,
So shall our souls embrace the light,
Becoming one, eternally,
In the vastness of the night.

From the mountain's peak to ocean's floor,
Each soul a drop, yet part of the whole,
In the river of becoming, we explore,
Together, we find our ultimate goal.

Traces of Holiness

In silence, holy traces lie,
In the laughter and in the tears,
In the moments that pass us by,
Echoing through the fleeting years.

Each breath a prayer, soft and sweet,
A testament of hope and grace,
In the humble, the lowly, the meek,
Resides the shining, sacred space.

Look closely, for the signs are clear,
In the kindness that we bestow,
In the love that draws us near,
The traces of holiness flow.

In the heartbeats shared in trust,
In the hands that lift others high,
Finding the beauty, as we must,
In the dance of the earth and sky.

Traces linger in every soul,
Reminders of the divine embrace,
In every gap, we find the whole,
And holiness reveals its face.

Unveiling the Sacred Script

In the scrolls of time, the truth is penned,
Each word a pathway to the light,
The sacred script, where hearts ascend,
Leading us from shadow to bright.

With reverence, we unfold the lines,
Finding echoes of our fate,
Each verse, a spark, divinely signs,
Guiding us to open the gate.

Through the ages, the message sings,
A chorus of wisdom, clear and bold,
In every heartbeat, the spirit brings,
Stories of love eternally told.

Let the words wash over your soul,
As we uncover each hidden gem,
In the tapestry, we are made whole,
Forever entwined, in the hymn.

In the heart, the knowledge ignites,
As the sacred script reveals its grace,
In unity, we find our heights,
In the embrace of the Creator's face.

Whispered Prayers of the Past

In quiet halls where candles burn,
Faint echoes of devotion yearn.
Soft whispers carried on the breeze,
A tapestry of faith that never frees.

Ancient words now softly fade,
In hearts of many, love cascades.
Each drop a promise, each sigh a plea,
A sacred bond, forever free.

The chime of hope, a bell's soft toll,
Connects the spirit, body, and soul.
Remembered grace in timeless prayer,
A sacred rhythm, forever shared.

Beneath the stars, in twilight's glow,
The faithful gather, hearts aglow.
In every prayer, a story we weave,
A legacy of love that we believe.

So let us speak in gentle tones,
In whispered prayers, love finds its homes.
Together we stand, hand in hand,
In the presence of the Divine, we stand.

Seasoned in the Light

In morning's grace, the dawn appears,
Revealing truth, soothing our fears.
Each golden ray a timeless guide,
Seasoned in light, we walk with pride.

With every breath, a call to share,
The wisdom found in earnest prayer.
Hearts aglow with eager grace,
In every smile, a sacred space.

Through trials faced and sorrows borne,
Hope rises bright with every morn.
As faithful souls, we lift our eyes,
To skies adorned where promise lies.

In twilight's glow, we gather near,
In shared stories, love draws clear.
To nourish hearts with words divine,
In light we find a love that shines.

So let us walk in paths of peace,
From joy to joy, our hearts increase.
Seasoned in love, with each embrace,
We find our place in endless grace.

Legacy of the Faithful

From ancestors' lips, sweet stories flow,
Of trials faced and seeds to sow.
Each moment cherished, wisdom grown,
In every heart, their love is shown.

The path they forged, a guiding light,
Through darkest nights and fiercest fight.
With every step, we carry forth,
Their legacy, a radiant worth.

In quiet deeds and whispered prayers,
We honor them, the faithful prayers.
The strength of many, forever bold,
In unity, their stories told.

With every trial, our spirits rise,
Awakening hope beneath the skies.
Each challenge met with faith renewed,
In love's embrace, we find our food.

Let gratitude bloom in fields of grace,
For those who walked, our firm embrace.
Together we stand, hand in hand,
Honoring faith across the land.

Ageless Reflections

In mirrors bright, the past reveals,
The echoes of our spirit's fields.
Every moment, a gentle guide,
In faith's embrace, we abide.

With each reflection, lessons seen,
In quiet corners where we've been.
Time weaving tales in silver thread,
Of hopes fulfilled and dreams long led.

From shadows cast in twilight's grace,
Emerges light in every place.
Ageless truths in whispers dwell,
Transforming hearts, a sacred swell.

The universe sings in unison,
A symphony of love begun.
With every breath and every prayer,
We find our strength, our longing there.

So here we stand, with souls ablaze,
Reflecting love in endless praise.
In ageless moments, dreams take flight,
Together, we journey towards the light.

The Evolution of Grace

From darkness born a gentle light,
A whisper calls, a sacred rite.
Through trials faced, our hearts embrace,
The hand of God, a gift of grace.

In humble prayers, in silent tears,
We find the strength to cast our fears.
With every step, His love persists,
In every soul, His warmth exists.

The past, a shadow, shapes our way,
Yet love endures, come what may.
In every heart, a story grows,
In every eye, His mercy flows.

We rise anew with every dawn,
In faith we journey, never drawn.
The evolution, love's sweet chase,
In every moment, we find grace.

A Symphony of Seasons

In spring's embrace, the flowers bloom,
God's canvas spreads from dusk to noon.
With every breeze, a promise sings,
Life awakens, hope takes wing.

Summer's warmth, the golden light,
Joy abounds, hearts shining bright.
In laughter shared, we find our way,
In love's embrace, we live the day.

Autumn's hush, the leaves of gold,
A fleeting moment, stories told.
In gentle winds, we feel the change,
God's faithfulness, forever strange.

Winter's call, a quiet peace,
In silent nights, our worries cease.
Through every season, time must flow,
A symphony of love we know.

Together we walk, hand in hand,
In life's embrace, together we stand.
A tapestry woven, divine design,
In every season, His love we find.

Covenant of the Ages

In ancient times, the promise made,
A sacred bond that will not fade.
Through every trial, through every tear,
A covenant shared, forever near.

The stars above, a witness bright,
To love's endurance, day and night.
In prayerful vows, our hearts unite,
A sacred oath, a guiding light.

Through floods and fires, we're held as one,
The journey forged, a race begun.
In every heartbeat, a legacy flows,
In every soul, the promise grows.

Though shadows loom and doubts arise,
In the embrace of faith, we rise.
The covenant strong, our spirits soar,
In every challenge, love restores.

Across the ages, voices blend,
A story woven, no end.
In sacred trust, we find our aim,
A covenant everlasting—His name.

The Spirit's Lament and Triumph

In shadows deep, the spirit weeps,
A longing heart, a silence keeps.
Through broken dreams and whispered fears,
A cry for hope in gathering years.

Yet in the dark, a light shall rise,
The dawn breaks forth, the spirit sighs.
For every tear, a promise blooms,
In every heart, His love consumes.

The trials faced, a sacred path,
In pain and sorrow, learn His wrath.
Yet through the storm, our spirits share,
A whispered prayer, a tender care.

And as we walk through valleys low,
The Triumph sung in every glow.
For in our hearts, His strength enshrined,
A spirit bold, a spirit blind.

So let the spirit dance in grace,
Through every trial, a sacred place.
In lament's deep, we find our song,
For in His arms, we all belong.

Sanctified Journey

In humble steps, we tread the path,
With faith our guide, escaping wrath.
Each prayer a whisper to the skies,
In sacred trust, our spirit flies.

Through trials and storms, we find our way,
The light of hope, brightens the day.
We seek His grace in every turn,
With every lesson, our hearts will learn.

In unity, our souls align,
One body, one spirit, divine design.
Through valleys low, we lift our eyes,
For in His love, our strength will rise.

The journey long, but never alone,
In faith, we find our true home.
Together we walk, side by side,
In the arms of Him, we abide.

With each step forth, our hearts will sing,
To the Father, our wandering King.
In every heartbeat, He is near,
In every moment, we feel no fear.

The Light of Persistence

In darkness deep, the light shines bold,
A beacon bright, a story told.
With every struggle, the flame ignites,
In hearts of courage, the spirit fights.

Faith like a river, flows through our veins,
In storms of doubt, it breaks the chains.
As shadows fade, His love ignites,
In every trials, hope ignites.

We stand together, hand in hand,
With truth our shield, we'll take a stand.
Through every setback, we rise again,
In the promise of light, we won't wane.

The path may tremble, the road be steep,
But in His arms, our souls He'll keep.
In the heart of struggle, we find our grace,
With every step, we'll seek His face.

Through every tear, there's strength to find,
In every trial, our hearts entwined.
For with each dawn, we rise anew,
In the arms of light, we're coming through.

Threads of the Heart

In tender threads, our stories weave,
A tapestry of love, we believe.
Each moment shared, a bond so true,
In the fabric of grace, we renew.

Through laughter shared and sorrows too,
In the garden of faith, our love will brew.
Each heart a note in the song of time,
In unity, our spirits climb.

As seasons change, we hold on tight,
In darkest hours, we find the light.
With hands entwined, we walk this road,
In every burden, we lift the load.

In whispers soft, our hopes conveyed,
In faith unyielding, our paths are laid.
Together we rise, together we stand,
In the threads of hope, His guiding hand.

For love's embrace, our hearts align,
In sacred trust, our lives entwine.
With every heartbeat, we shall impart,
The endless journey of every heart.

Within the Cradle of Time

In the cradle of time, our souls reside,
With every moment, He's by our side.
The echoes of ages call our name,
In His embrace, we'll never be the same.

With every sunrise, the promise wakes,
In the still of dawn, our spirit aches.
In sacred whispers, wisdom flows,
Within the heart, His light bestows.

Through trials faced, we grow and learn,
In every heartbeat, His love returns.
With courage unyielding, our destinies blend,
In the cradle of time, we transcend.

Each memory held, a treasure rare,
In every sorrow, we find His care.
The tapestry woven, our lives entwined,
Within the cradle, His peace we find.

So let us cherish this sacred gift,
In the bond of faith, our spirits lift.
Through ages gone and those to come,
Within His love, we are forever one.

Maturity of the Spirit

In silence, the soul learns to grow,
As time weaves its wisdom in gentle flow.
Through trials and joys, we seek the light,
Transforming the darkness, embracing the night.

With patience, we walk on a sacred road,
Each step a lesson, a humble ode.
The spirit ascends, like a dove in flight,
Bringing forth truths that shine ever bright.

Forgiveness blooms in the heart's warm place,
Like petals of grace in the softest space.
In surrender, we find our true worth,
In the garden of faith, we're reborn on Earth.

Love is the anchor in turbulent seas,
Guiding our hearts with a whispering breeze.
The spirit matures as we learn to share,
The gifts of the heavens, the love that we bear.

In the end of our journey, as shadows blend,
We find all our paths converge, transcend.
Maturity of spirit, a glorious decree,
To dwell forever in the Light we see.

The Pathway of Providence

Upon this pathway, divine and wide,
We walk with faith, and never with pride.
Each step is guided, each road we take,
A tapestry woven, for love's own sake.

In whispers soft, the heart will hear,
The call of the heavens, the presence near.
Through valleys low and mountains high,
The hand of Providence will never lie.

In times of trouble, in moments of grace,
We find the embrace of a holy place.
Trust in the journey, though shadows may fall,
For love is the promise that conquers all.

With each dawn rising, an angel shows,
The way to the light where true knowledge grows.
The pathway unfolds with each humble prayer,
Leading us forward, divinely aware.

As stars in the night lead sailors at sea,
Providence guides, setting our spirits free.
Each step in the dance of this earthly place,
We're cradled in mercy, surrounded by grace.

Echoes of the Divine Heart

In the stillness, a whisper calls,
Through the echoes where love never falls.
Hearts intertwined in a heavenly song,
Resonating with grace, where we all belong.

In the tapestry pure, God's love laid bare,
Every thread woven with tender care.
We feel the pulse of the divine's embrace,
In the quiet moments, we share a space.

Each heartbeat reflects the celestial rhyme,
Reminding us gently of love's endless climb.
In the dance of creation, our spirits entwine,
Echoing notes of the heart's pure design.

As rivers flow into the vast, deep sea,
So too do we merge, striving to be free.
The sacred connection that binds us all tight,
Holds us together in love's radiant light.

In the laughter, in tears, in the still of the night,
The echoes resound, making shadows take flight.
Divine is the heart that beats with our own,
A symphony woven, never alone.

Serpent and Dove: A Parable

In the garden, the serpent waits low,
Whispered temptations, a subtle foe.
The dove, so pure, takes to the sky,
Guiding us gently, to strive and to fly.

The dance of the cunning, the light and the dark,
A lesson of choices, of love's quiet spark.
In wisdom, we see what the serpent unfolds,
Yet strength lies in mercy, in stories retold.

The heart of the dove, a beacon of grace,
Invites us to seek a heavenly place.
With courage to stand, when shadows appear,
Embracing the truth, rejecting the fear.

Each moment a battle, each choice to be made,
In the tapestry rich, by love conveyed.
The serpent may hiss, but the dove soars above,
Bound by the promise of eternal love.

Let us reflect, on the paths that we take,
With love as our armor, we willingly break.
For in every struggle, the light will renew,
Serpent and dove, both play their due.

Reverence in Change

In seasons' shift we find our grace,
Each leaf that falls, a sacred trace.
The wind whispers soft, a gentle guide,
In nature's hand, we abide.

With every dawn, new hope is born,
The light reveals, the shadows mourn.
Embrace the path that fate has laid,
In faithfulness, our hearts are swayed.

The river flows, it knows no end,
Through stones and bends, it dares descend.
Each current teaches, a lesson clear,
In the quiet flow, we draw near.

Transformation sings in every soul,
With every change, we become whole.
In the tapestry of days gone by,
A sacred thread, we testify.

So let us walk in reverence deep,
In every moment, the truth we keep.
In change we see the hand of God,
A journey blessed, our paths will trod.

Time's Sacred Embrace

With ticking clocks, the moments weave,
A tapestry of those who believe.
Each tick, a prayer, each tock, a song,
In time's embrace, we all belong.

The past unfolds its gentle hand,
A map of love through shifting sand.
In memories cherished, we find our way,
Guided by light of yesterday.

As seasons pass, like waves that roll,
Each heartbeat whispers of the whole.
In sacred rhythm, souls entwine,
In time's soft glow, the light will shine.

So let us honor the fleeting grace,
In every moment, seek His face.
For time, though swift, is not in vain,
In sacred trust, we bear our gain.

In every hour, His love we trace,
In time's embrace, we find our place.
With every breath, eternity calls,
In the sacred dance, the spirit sprawls.

Trials of the Heart

In the valley, shadows grow,
Yet faith ignites a silent glow.
Through trials fierce, our spirit bends,
In every struggle, love transcends.

The thorns we bear, they teach us peace,
In brokenness, our strength will lease.
For every tear that stains the ground,
A seed of hope in grace is found.

Through darkness deep, the light will shine,
In every wound, His hand aligns.
In the rugged path, our hearts renounce,
The burdens held, we must denounce.

So let us trust in hands unseen,
With weary hearts, to rise between.
For trials shape the soul awake,
In every heartache, change we make.

In love we find the way to mend,
Through trials of the heart, we tend.
With every step, in faith we trod,
Through storms we brave, we seek our God.

The Wisdom of Years

In silence deep, the wisdom grows,
With every wrinkle, the story flows.
Through trials faced and victories won,
The light of years shines like the sun.

In gentle words, the truth is found,
With lessons learned, the heart is crowned.
Each moment shared, the laughter rings,
In life's embrace, the spirit sings.

Remembered joys, the love we spread,
In every tear, the heart is fed.
Through wisdom's lens, the past relives,
In gratitude, our spirit gives.

So let us cherish the days we've known,
In timeless grace, our seeds are sown.
For ages pass, yet still we stand,
With open hearts, we heed His hand.

In the wisdom of the years we find,
A deeper love that binds mankind.
In every story, His truth will soar,
With each embrace, we're evermore.

Forged in the Fires of Patience

In the stillness of the night, we pray,
Hearts ignited, led on our way.
Through trials deep, our spirits rise,
In faith unshaken, we seek the skies.

Each moment waits, a lesson learned,
In embers bright, our souls are turned.
Forged like steel, renewed and strong,
In patience, we find where we belong.

The furnace hot, it shapes our soul,
With every struggle, we become whole.
In quiet trust, we walk the path,
Found in the warmth of divine wrath.

Through every tear, through every sigh,
We learn to live, we learn to die.
In trials, grace does softly flow,
From patience, the spirit learns to grow.

As we endure, our hopes ignite,
Forged anew, we embrace the light.
In fire's dance, our dreams expand,
Embracing all that He has planned.

Ascending Dreams

Up towards the heavens, our hopes take flight,
Bathed in the glow of celestial light.
With hearts aligned, we reach for grace,
In each gentle whisper, we find our place.

The stars above, a guiding song,
Lifting us high, where we belong.
In every trial, a promise gleams,
In faith we rise, to chase our dreams.

Through valleys deep, our spirits soar,
In love's embrace, we're forevermore.
Each step we take, in trust we stand,
Together we walk, hand in hand.

Awake our hearts to visions bright,
In shadows cast, we find the light.
Each dream a thread, woven with care,
A tapestry rich, in the moment shared.

With open arms, we receive the call,
In unity strong, we will not fall.
As horizons stretch, the skies reveal,
Ascending dreams, we learn to heal.

The Divine Weaving

In the loom of life, our threads intertwine,
Stitched by the hand of the One divine.
Each color bright, a story to tell,
In patterns of hope, we weave so well.

With silken strands of joy and pain,
The tapestry holds our love and rain.
Every tear drops, a shimmering bead,
In heart's gentle folds, we plant the seed.

The weaver guides with sacred care,
In every twist, the breath of prayer.
As shadows fall and light breaks through,
In the sacred weave, we start anew.

From chaos born, a masterpiece grows,
In the hands of time, true beauty shows.
Listeners hear the heartbeat's drum,
In the fabric of faith, we are all one.

In the light of dawn, our spirits rise,
Bound by the threads of the endless skies.
For love is the pattern, hope is the seam,
In the divine weaving, we live our dream.

Hope's Endurance

Upon the altar of weary souls,
We gather strength, as the spirit consoles.
In darkest nights, hope whispers clear,
A gentle promise that draws us near.

With every storm, a lesson comes,
In faith we march, while the world hums.
The heart still beats, though shadows loom,
In the garden of grace, flowers bloom.

Through trials faced, our courage swells,
In valleys low, the echo dwells.
With open arms, we hold the flame,
A beacon bright, we call His name.

The path may twist, but we stand strong,
In unity's song, we all belong.
Through every ache, with love we cope,
For in our faith lies the seed of hope.

As dawn breaks forth, our spirits rise,
Transcending pain, we touch the skies.
Hope's endurance is a sacred shield,
In love's embrace, we are healed.

Remnants of Eternity

In the silence of the stars, they call,
Whispers of love in the cosmic hall.
With every breath, we touch the divine,
In shadows of time, our souls entwine.

The echoes of faith, a guiding light,
In the darkest hour, shining bright.
Threads of the past into the now,
In the tapestry of life, we bow.

In the gardens of hope, we plant our dreams,
Flowing like rivers, like silver streams.
The remnants we cherish, both near and far,
They pulsate within like a morning star.

Embrace the beauty, the sacred grace,
In every heartbeat, a holy trace.
Together we wander, hand in hand,
Upon the whispers of the ancient land.

With every dawn, a chance to renew,
In the language of love, forever true.
For in the end, we are but one,
Remnants of eternity, under the sun.

The Path Awaits

Upon the mountain's edge we stand,
Gazing forth to a promised land.
With every step, the spirit lifts,
Guided by faith, the heart gifts.

Through valleys low and rivers wide,
In the embrace of the Fates, we bide.
Each twist and turn, a lesson learned,
In the dance of life, we are discerned.

The path ahead, both bright and clear,
Echoes of blessings, whispers near.
With courage as our steadfast light,
We journey forth to reclaim the night.

In the moments still, a voice we hear,
A song of hope, dispelling fear.
So onward, beloved, with hearts ablaze,
For the path awaits, in grace we raise.

Together we'll tread, the sacred ground,
In the sacred silence, love abounds.
For on this path, we find our song,
In unity's strength, forever strong.

Unfurling Petals of Grace

In the morning light, petals unfold,
Stories of love in hues of gold.
Each flower a prayer, each bloom a wish,
A dance of the heart, like a sacred kiss.

In gardens of faith, the colors blend,
A tapestry woven, where spirits mend.
With whispers of hope upon the breeze,
In every moment, our souls find ease.

The fragrance of joy, it fills the air,
In every heartbeat, a tender care.
As nature's hymn sings soft and low,
We embrace the grace that we all know.

In the arms of beauty, we find release,
In every petal, a glimpse of peace.
Together we gather, in love's embrace,
Unfurling the petals of eternal grace.

With every sunrise, the promise gleams,
In the silent night, we dare to dream.
For in the garden of life's embrace,
We bloom forever in boundless grace.

Against the Winds of Change

In turbulent times, we stand our ground,
With faith as our anchor, hope is found.
The winds may howl, the storm may rage,
Yet in our hearts, we turn the page.

Each challenge faced, a lesson learned,
In the fires of trial, our spirit burned.
With every whisper, the truth will rise,
Against the winds, we touch the skies.

In storms of doubt, we find our way,
With love as our light, we won't dismay.
Through tempests fierce, our souls take flight,
In unity's strength, we embrace the light.

With every battle, we are reborn,
In resilience' embrace, we shall not mourn.
Together we sail, through seas unknown,
Against the winds, we are not alone.

For in the midst of chaos, we will stand,
With hearts united, hand in hand.
In the dance of change, our spirits grow,
Against the winds, our love will flow.

Beneath the Surface

In whispers soft, the waters flow,
Beneath the surface, truth does grow.
A silent prayer, unseen by eyes,
Where faith resides and spirit flies.

The depths conceal, yet hearts can see,
The sacred dance of life's decree.
For in the dark, the seed is sown,
And in the stillness, love is grown.

Awake the soul, let courage rise,
As dawn breaks forth, the promise lies.
With every ripple, wisdom speaks,
In quietude, the heart then seeks.

Though storms may rage upon the tide,
The whispered hope shall be my guide.
For in the depths, the light shines bright,
And leads the way through darkest night.

So trust the path, though hidden still,
For under waves, there dwells a will.
A testament to what is true,
Beneath the surface, faith renews.

Seasons of Abiding

In spring, the blooms awaken dreams,
A gift of grace in sunlit beams.
With every bud, a promise made,
In seasons' arms, divinely laid.

Summer warms the heart's embrace,
With laughter bright, in sacred space.
The days unfold like tender leaves,
In joy and love, the spirit weaves.

As autumn whispers, change is near,
The vibrant hues remind us here.
With gratitude, we gather close,
In fading light, we cherish most.

Winter's chill brings peace serene,
In quietude, the soul can glean.
Through frosty nights, the stars align,
In every season, love divine.

In cycles spun with sacred grace,
We find our place, we seek His face.
For every turn, a chance to grow,
In seasons of abiding, hearts aglow.

Intentions through Time

Upon the altar, candles burn,
With cada flame, a prayer's return.
In moments still, intentions rise,
As echoes reach the boundless skies.

Each heartbeat marks the sacred flow,
A river deep where blessings grow.
Through every choice, a path defined,
In whispers soft, the soul aligned.

Past shadows linger, teach us well,
In every trial, we learn to dwell.
When hope seems lost, the spirit yearns,
In every lesson, wisdom turns.

For time's embrace, a timeless gift,
In gratitude, our spirits lift.
With love as guide, we walk so bold,
In intentions set, our truth unfolds.

With open hearts, we cast our aims,
In life's design, we play our games.
Eternity awaits the line,
As we create, His love divine.

The Serpent and the Rose

In the garden, shadows weave,
With whispers sweet, the heart believes.
The serpent coils, with charm and guise,
But in the rose, the truth shall rise.

Amidst the thorns, a beauty stands,
In petals soft, God's loving hands.
Though tempests rise, and doubts may swarm,
In every trial, He keeps us warm.

The dance of light and dark entwined,
In every choice, the heart aligned.
Resist the call of endless night,
For in the rose, we find the light.

Each breath a testament of grace,
In trials faced, we find our place.
Beyond the serpent's silken lies,
The rose will bloom, love never dies.

So heed the call, embrace the light,
In every challenge, stand and fight.
For in the garden, love has grown,
The serpent fades, the rose, our own.

Stones of Remembrance

Upon the mountain high, we stand,
Each stone a tale, each grain a hand.
Whispers of the ancients, they call,
Their lessons, precious, we recall.

Cradled in faith, our spirits rise,
In silence found beneath the skies.
The echoes speak of love and grace,
In this sacred, hallowed place.

These stones, reminders of our way,
Guide us in light, through night and day.
For every heart that seeks the truth,
Find solace here, regain your youth.

A pathway forged in trials past,
Through challenges, our bonds hold fast.
In unity, we raise our psalms,
Together, find our healing balms.

The mountains whisper low and clear,
In reverence, we draw near.
Each stone a witness to our plight,
In faith, we walk, through darkest night.

Growth in Solitude

In the quiet of the lone retreat,
Where whispers dance and shadows meet.
We find the strength to face our fears,
In solitude, we shed our tears.

The heart, in silence, learns to bloom,
In sacred space, dispelling gloom.
With every breath, the soul unfolds,
In whispered truths, our fate beholds.

Each moment cherished in the still,
A timeless grace, a gentle thrill.
The Spirit breathes, within us, sighs,
In solitude, our purpose lies.

In depths of silence, wisdom grows,
As nature's light, within us, glows.
From barren ground, the seed will rise,
In quietude, the heart complies.

So let us dwell where silence reigns,
Finding peace within the chains.
For in this space, our spirits soar,
In growth, we seek forevermore.

Echoes of the Ancients

In the stillness of the night so deep,
The ancients' whispers softly creep.
A tapestry of wisdom spun,
In echoes past, our journey's begun.

Through valleys wide and mountains tall,
Their stories weave, uniting all.
In sacred texts, their truths abide,
In every heart, they do reside.

From fires of old, their flames still glow,
Illuminating paths we know.
As haunted winds through branches sway,
They guide us gently on our way.

In every stone, their spirit's found,
In laughter sweet, in sorrow's sound.
We listen close, their lessons clear,
In every heartbeat, they draw near.

So gather round the hearth tonight,
In unity, embrace the light.
For in the echoes, we are blessed,
In ancient truth, we find our rest.

With Each Passing Dawn

With each new dawn, the light does break,
In golden rays, our souls awake.
A sacred gift from realms above,
A gentle nudge, a push of love.

With every sunrise, hope is sown,
In tender moments, we have grown.
The brush of light on weary brow,
Reminding us of here and now.

In colors vibrant, skies ablaze,
We find our path through morning haze.
Each day a chance, each moment pure,
In faith, we stand, in joy, we endure.

Let gratitude fill every breath,
For in this life, there is no death.
In spirit's rise, we find our song,
With each dawn's grace, we all belong.

So welcome, day, and all you bring,
In sacred rhythm, let us sing.
For in these hours, we weave the thread,
Of love and light, in peace, we're led.

Celestial Growth

In the garden of the skies, we bloom,
Roots entwined with love's sweet grace.
Each star a whisper, bright to loom,
Guiding hearts in sacred space.

With every dawn, a promise lies,
Nurtured by the sun's warm glow.
Faith unyielding, as we rise,
In the dance of life, we grow.

Through tears we learn, through pain we thrive,
Branches stretching, reaching wide.
In this path, our spirits drive,
Finding light that turns the tide.

Among the clouds, the spirit sings,
Echoes soft in twilight's fold.
With open hearts, we seek the wings,
Celestial truths, timeless and bold.

In the cycle, endless grace,
Life and death, a sacred flow.
As we journey, we embrace,
The everlasting beauty we sow.

Harmonies of the Old

Ancient whispers fill the air,
Voices echo from the past.
In their stories, wisdom rare,
Guiding us, steadfast and fast.

Through the ages, songs resound,
Melodies of truth profound.
In their harmonies, we are found,
A sacred bond, forever bound.

From the mountains to the sea,
Nature's chorus weaves and flows.
In the rustle of the tree,
Olden rhythms softly grow.

As the moonlight bathes the night,
We gather round the fire's glow.
Sharing tales in soft twilight,
Harvesting what elders know.

With each note, our spirits rise,
Unity in every chord.
In the harmony of the skies,
We find solace, blessed and adored.

Unfolding in Time

Like petals opening to light,
We unfold with gentle grace.
Moments sculpted, pure and bright,
Each heartbeat finds its place.

In silence, wisdom starts to bloom,
Echoes of a sacred rhyme.
Trusting purpose, dispelling gloom,
We embrace the flow of time.

Threads of fate weave, intertwine,
Every breath a step divine.
In the tapestry we find,
Life's design, a grand design.

Seasons change but love remains,
In the cycle, hope shall shine.
Through the trials and the rains,
Faith endures, a vibrant line.

As we journey, light shall guide,
Revealing paths once hidden,
In our hearts, the truth resides,
Unfolding wisdom, brightly written.

Divine Lessons of Resilience

In shadows cast, a lesson learned,
Through the storms and trials we face.
From ashes, new desires burned,
Rising up with steadfast grace.

Strength within, a quiet fire,
Nurtured by the trials we bear.
With each struggle, hearts aspire,
Finding peace in earnest prayer.

In the depths of every fall,
A whisper calls us to arise.
With every tear, we hear the call,
A light that shines beyond the skies.

For every wound, a story told,
Of courage found in tender hearts.
In every challenge, we behold,
The gift of faith that never departs.

As we walk this path of grace,
Finding strength in every trial,
In every moment, embrace
The divine lessons that make us whole.

Embracing Divine Evolution

In whispers of grace, we grow anew,
Transforming hearts, with love imbued.
Each moment a gift, a sacred dance,
In every trial, we find our chance.

The spirit ascends, like mist in the light,
Guided by faith through the darkest night.
Hands raised in praise, we seek to see,
The path unfolding, our destiny.

With every breath, we shed our fear,
Embracing the change, the voice is clear.
Awakening souls to the depths of grace,
Journeying onward, we find our place.

In harmony's song, we find the key,
Unlocking the love in you and me.
Divine evolution, a promise so bright,
We walk in His shadow, guided by light.

Together we rise, in unity's call,
Embracing the love that embraces all.
In the silence, we hear the truth,
Awakening spirit, eternal youth.

The Tree of Life Expands

Beneath the skies, the tree takes root,
Branches reaching, life's pursuit.
In every leaf, a story told,
Of love and strength, of hearts so bold.

With roots entwined, our spirits blend,
A tapestry woven, no end to mend.
In sacred whispers, the winds do play,
The tree of life grows, come what may.

Seasons change, yet strength remains,
Through storms and sunshine, joy and pains.
Every blossom brings forth the new,
In shared embrace, our love shines through.

Fruits of labor, sweet and ripe,
Harvesting grace, our spirits hype.
All around, the beauty spreads,
In unity's light, our soul is fed.

As we gather, in circles wide,
The tree of life, our sacred guide.
Together we stand, together we thrive,
In love's embrace, we truly arrive.

Sunrise Over Yesterday

In dawn's embrace, we find the way,
Shedding shadows of yesterday.
With colors bright, the skies ignite,
A canvas of hope, pure and bright.

Each ray that breaks is a promise made,
Wiping the slate, and fears do fade.
In every heartbeat, a new refrain,
Carrying forward the lessons gained.

As morning lifts the veil of night,
Our spirits dance in joyful flight.
Let the past go, in faith we trust,
In love we rise, in hope we must.

With every step, we cherish grace,
Embracing the dawn, we find our place.
The sun beside us, forever shines,
Guiding our path, where true love aligns.

In the light of day, we stand as one,
Celebrating the journey, each race we run.
For every sunrise, a chance to renew,
A bright tomorrow awaits me and you.

The Unseen Timekeeper

In silence dwells the gentle hand,
That guides us softly, through life's vast land.
The unseen timekeeper, wise and true,
Counting moments, for me and for you.

With every tick, a heartbeat felt,
In every lapse, the lessons dealt.
In shadows cast, the truth reveals,
The quiet whispers, our soul it heals.

Invisible threads, connecting us all,
In love's embrace, we rise and fall.
For in the stillness, we find our way,
The unseen timekeeper, come what may.

As seasons change, and years unfold,
The stories written, in hearts of gold.
In patience's grace, we learn to be,
Trusting the path, so wild and free.

In every second, a spark divine,
Reminding us of the grand design.
Through every heartbeat, we're intertwined,
Forever moving, the sacred mind.

Time's Sacred Tapestry

In the stillness, time unwinds,
Threads of fate in the divine,
Moments woven, hearts entwined,
Each tick a whisper from the shrine.

Joy and sorrow, joys and woes,
In every season, God's grace flows,
A tapestry of life that grows,
With every stitch, the spirit knows.

Past and future, intertwined,
Sacred echoes, love defined,
In the silence, hearts aligned,
A holy truth in every mind.

With reverence, we watch the loom,
Creation swells, dispels the gloom,
Each thread a prayer, each moment bloom,
In time's embrace, we find our room.

So let us dance in space and time,
In holy rhythms, pure and prime,
For in our hearts, the bells will chime,
Forever bound in love's sweet rhyme.

Ascending the Mountain of Faith

With each step, we rise above,
The trials faced, the bonds of love,
Each breath a prayer, a gentle shove,
As we seek the guidance from above.

The path is steep, yet hearts are light,
In shadows deep, we find the light,
Together as one, we'll take the flight,
Embracing faith, our spirits bright.

Among the stones, the wildflowers bloom,
In their fragrance, dispels the gloom,
Each summit gained brings forth its room,
Where hope is born and doubts consume.

In the whispers of the mountain's age,
We find the wisdom, the sacred sage,
Hearts in union, turning the page,
With every struggle, we disengage.

Upon the peak, our souls take wing,
In harmony, we rise and sing,
For in our hearts, the angels bring,
A sacred truth in love's own ring.

The Everlasting Embrace

In the quiet, a love appears,
Wrapping tightly, calming fears,
A warm embrace through all the years,
In every joy, in every tear.

Through trials faced, we stand as one,
In darkness deep, the light has shone,
With open hearts, we have begun,
To know the grace of the Divine Son.

In the silence, His voice we hear,
As shadows fade, all becomes clear,
With every step, He draws us near,
In faith's embrace, we persevere.

Beneath the stars, the heavens' gaze,
Illuminate our spiritual ways,
In whispered prayers, we count the days,
Each breath a promise, love displays.

Together still, our spirits rise,
As boundless love fills up the skies,
In the embrace of endless ties,
We find our home, our true replies.

Chronicles of the Soul

In every heartbeat, stories lie,
Chronicles whispered, spirits sigh,
An eternal quest, the heart's comply,
To seek the truth that never dies.

With every dawn, a page will turn,
In the depths of love, we learn,
A sacred fire, a constant burn,
With every choice, the soul can yearn.

Through laughter shared, through tears we shed,
In every moment, the Spirit led,
We weave the tale, the life we tread,
In faith's embrace, we're gently fed.

In shadows cast, the light breaks forth,
In every challenge, we find our worth,
With every struggle, a rebirth,
Uniting souls, the endless mirth.

So let us write, our hearts as ink,
With faith and love, we find the link,
In every thought, our spirits sync,
In the chronicles, we never sink.

The Woven Tapestry

In threads of gold and whispers bright,
A story spins, a sacred night.
Each life entwined, a sacred art,
Together we weave, from soul to heart.

Through trials faced and love embraced,
We find our strength, our faith, our grace.
With every knot, a tale is sewn,
In this grand cloth, we are not alone.

The fibers stretch, the colors blend,
In harmony parts, we grasp the end.
The unseen hand guides every thread,
In this tapestry, the spirit's bred.

As seasons change and shadows play,
Hope shines again with the break of day.
Every stitch, a prayer unspoken,
In the woven tapestry, love's token.

Together we rise, together we stand,
In moments shared, faith in hand.
For through the patterns, divinity's mark,
In the woven tapestry, we find our spark.

Grit in the Gloaming

When twilight falls on weary lands,
The heart holds firm as hope withstands.
In whispered prayers, strength is found,
Grit in the gloaming, a sacred ground.

With shadows long and spirits high,
We seek the stars in the darkened sky.
Each step we take, though weary, bold,
In faith's embrace, our stories told.

Through silent tears and laughter bright,
We walk the path toward the light.
Though dusk may linger, dawn shall rise,
In the grit of gloaming, our faith replies.

For in the struggles, lessons learned,
A flicker of warmth, our hearts have burned.
With every moment, we shall prevail,
For love's endurance will never fail.

So as we tread 'neath fading sun,
We cherish the battles that we've won.
In the twilight's glow, we shall stand tall,
Grit in the gloaming, we answer the call.

Faithful Shadows

In the stillness of the night,
Faithful shadows take to flight.
They dance upon the silent ground,
In every heartbeat, love is found.

Beneath the moon's soft, gentle glow,
Whispers of truth begin to flow.
In every corner, grace is near,
Faithful shadows banish fear.

Through trials thick and valleys deep,
In the arms of night, our souls we keep.
With every light, a promise made,
In faithful shadows, our path is laid.

Amidst the darkness, hope can rise,
With silent prayers to the skies.
For even when the world feels cold,
Faithful shadows hold the bold.

Together we walk, hand in hand,
Through the valleys of shifting sand.
In shadows' embrace, we find our way,
Faithful and true, come what may.

Beyond the Sands of Hours

Time drifts on like grains of sand,
Each moment whispers, by faith we stand.
For what is life but fleeting breath,
In every heartbeat, there's a depth.

Beyond the sands where shadows play,
Our spirits soar, come what may.
In every tick, a chance we seize,
In love and faith, we find our ease.

Through trials faced and dreams we chase,
We gather strength in every place.
With every dawn, the light renews,
Beyond the sands, we find the clues.

For in the whispers of the night,
The soul ignites with love's true light.
Every grain holds a sacred vow,
In the embrace of the here and now.

So let us heed the call of time,
In every rhythm, a sacred rhyme.
Beyond the sands, in spirit, we soar,
A journey of love, forevermore.

The Alchemy of Faith

In shadows deep, where doubts reside,
The heart seeks light, with hope as guide.
A whisper soft, a promise clear,
Transforms the soul, dispels the fear.

With every prayer, a spark ignites,
In darkest nights, the spirit fights.
Each tear a gem, each sigh a stone,
In faith's embrace, we're never alone.

The hands of grace weave love's great thread,
Harmony born from the spirits led.
Through trials faced, the truths unfold,
Faith's gold shines bright, more than foretold.

So trust the path, though winding still,
In every challenge, find God's will.
The alchemy of love takes form,
In faith's pure fire, we are reborn.

Let gratitude flow like rivers wide,
In every heartbeat, let joy abide.
For in this dance of life and grace,
We find our home, a sacred space.

A Pilgrimage of Patience

Beneath the sun, our journey starts,
With faith as compass, love as hearts.
Each step we take, a lesson learned,
In patience' arms, our spirits yearn.

Through valleys low and mountains high,
With every prayer, the soul can fly.
The road is long, but truth aligns,
In every pause, the heart divines.

The twisted paths of doubt and fear,
Are guided by a voice so dear.
With gentle hands, the moment holds,
Our spirits soar, as patience unfolds.

For in the wait, the heart finds grace,
In silence deep, the souls embrace.
Each breath a prayer, each pause a sign,
The pilgrimage, our spirits twine.

So onward still, through night and day,
In faith we'll walk, come what may.
With every trial, our trust will grow,
A pilgrimage, where love will flow.

Echoing Blessings Through Time

In every dawn, a blessing wakes,
The light reveals what love creates.
Each heartbeat echoes past and near,
A symphony of grace we hear.

Through ages old, the lessons call,
In every rise, in every fall.
The tapestry of life unspools,
With threads of faith, weaving life's rules.

In whispered prayers, the echoes sound,
A circle wide, where love is found.
Time holds the stories, both sweet and deep,
In blessings shared, our hearts we keep.

So gather close, let kindness reign,
Through trials faced, through joy and pain.
For every echo, a light will spark,
Through time's embrace, we leave our mark.

From ages past, to futures bright,
Our spirits soar in love's pure light.
With every blessing, we entwine,
Echoing grace through space and time.

The Sacred Echo

In sacred spaces, silence breathes,
Where hearts unveil their quiet needs.
A gentle echo calls our name,
In shadows sweet, we find the flame.

With every sigh, a prayer ascends,
In whispered hopes, our spirit mends.
The sacred pulse, like waves will flow,
Connecting souls, where love will grow.

Through nature's hymn, the angels sing,
The sacred echoes, life they bring.
In every rustle, in every breeze,
A touch of grace, the heart's release.

So pause and listen, hear the sound,
In every heart, the echo found.
For in this dance of love's delight,
The sacred echo shines so bright.

Embrace the stillness, let it be,
In every moment, find the key.
For in the quiet, peace will flow,
And reveal the path where love can grow.

The Metamorphosis of the Heart

In silence, whispers of the soul,
A heart once heavy, now made whole.
Through trials fierce, a light breaks free,
A sacred journey, transforming me.

In shadows deep, the Spirit learns,
From ashes rise, a fire burns.
With every tear, a lesson gained,
In love's embrace, we are sustained.

The chrysalis, a sacred space,
Where courage finds its rightful place.
In faith's sweet grace, the heart will soar,
A boundless gift, forevermore.

As dawn unfolds, the darkness fades,
With every step, a new life wades.
In hearts of gold, the truth is found,
A symphony of joy profound.

In gratitude, we lift our voice,
For every pain has led to choice.
The metamorphosis guides our way,
In love's pure light, we choose to stay.

Eternal Bloom

In gardens blessed by morning's light,
Where petals dance, and souls take flight.
Each blossom sings of grace divine,
In beauty's gaze, our hearts align.

With every breath, the Spirit grows,
A sacred bond that softly glows.
In seasons rough, we learn to trust,
For in our hearts, there's love, not dust.

In whispered prayers, the flowers share,
The essence of hope, forever rare.
A fragrance sweet, a promise clear,
In every bloom, our path is near.

Through storms and trials, the roots run deep,
In gentle hands, our harvest we reap.
With gratitude, we tend the land,
Eternal bloom, by grace we stand.

As twilight falls, the stars ignite,
Each petal glistens in soft twilight.
In nature's song, we find our room,
In love's embrace, our souls in bloom.

Spirit's Resilience

Through valleys dark, the spirit calls,
A gentle voice that never falls.
In trials faced, we learn to rise,
With faith as wings, we touch the skies.

Each burden borne, a treasure found,
In every loss, a strength unbound.
Through storms that rage, the soul will dance,
In every challenge, there's a chance.

The fire within, it fuels our quest,
In courage found, we find our rest.
With every breath, resilience grows,
In love's embrace, the spirit glows.

With open hearts, we walk the trail,
In grace we stand, we shall not fail.
For in the trials, a truth will sing,
The spirit shines, our offering.

In unity, we gather near,
With voices strong, we cast out fear.
In hope's warm light, our dreams ascend,
Through spirit's strength, we shall transcend.

Carved by Seasons

In autumn's breeze, the leaves will fall,
Each crumbling moment hears the call.
For every season has its song,
In nature's rhythm, we belong.

The winter's chill, a pause divine,
In stillness deep, the heart will shine.
From frost we learn, to cherish warmth,
In quiet trust, the soul transforms.

As spring awakens from her sleep,
With colors bright, new promises leap.
In budding dreams, we place our faith,
In every bloom, the heart feels safe.

The summer's glow, a radiant dance,
In laughter shared, we take a chance.
With every heartbeat, life renews,
In love's embrace, we find our muse.

Through cycles vast, we find our way,
In every season, night and day.
Carved by time, our hearts will sing,
In harmony, joy flowers and brings.

The Prism of Divine Growth

In shadows cast by sacred light,
A seedling stirs in silent night,
Each petal whispering its name,
In colors bright, it seeks the flame.

From soil blessed with holy grace,
It reaches up in warm embrace,
With every trial, it learns to bloom,
Transforming pain, dispelling gloom.

In every storm, it finds its way,
Each raindrop's gift, a chance to sway,
The sun will rise, the dawn will break,
And in the light, new dreams awake.

From root to branch, a dance of trust,
In faith's embrace, we grow robust,
Each sigh of wind, a gentle prayer,
The prism sparkles, love laid bare.

A tapestry of life unfolds,
In every hue, a tale retold,
The light of heaven guides the mind,
Divine growth seeks the heart aligned.

A Journey Beyond

With every step on sacred ground,
The echoes of the lost resound,
In whispers soft, the path does call,
To journey forth, to rise, not fall.

Through valleys low and mountains high,
In shadows deep beneath the sky,
Faith lights the way, a guiding star,
Each moment cherished, near or far.

Altar stones where dreams reside,
In search of truth, we find our pride,
With open hearts, our spirits soar,
A journey beyond, forevermore.

The rivers flow with stories old,
Of wanderers, brave and bold,
In every wave, a new release,
A journey blessed, a quest for peace.

The horizon calls, a vibrant hue,
Beyond the known, the first step true,
With faith as compass, we will roam,
A journey beyond, to find our home.

Illuminated Steps

In twilight's grace, we find our way,
Each step a prayer, come what may,
The whispers of the past draw near,
Illuminated paths, crystal clear.

With courage held, we walk this road,
Trusting the light, releasing the load,
In every heartbeat, the sacred beats,
Illuminated steps, our spirit greets.

Beyond the veil of doubt and fear,
The truth emerges, ever clear,
In every moment, love revealed,
Illuminated steps, our fate sealed.

Through trials faced and lessons learned,
A flame of hope, forever burned,
With open eyes, we seek the blessed,
Illuminated steps, our souls rest.

So walk with grace, with joy, with love,
As stars above guide us from above,
On this journey, we lift our hands,
Illuminated steps through sacred lands.

Prayers Woven in Time

In silence shared, we weave our dreams,
With threads of faith in sacred seams,
Each whispered sigh, a tapestry,
Prayers woven in time, eternally.

The fabric of love, so richly spun,
We gather hope as day is done,
Each heart a note in the grand design,
Prayers woven in time, so divine.

Through tears and laughter, we unite,
In darkness found, we seek the light,
With hands held high, our voices climb,
Prayers woven in time, a holy rhyme.

In every corner of this Earth,
Resounds the song of sacred birth,
In every soul, a dream to climb,
Prayers woven in time, love's chime.

So gather close, let spirits rise,
In unity, we touch the skies,
With each heartbeat, a sacred line,
Prayers woven in time, the stars align.

Mosaic of the Soul

In fragments we gather, a tapestry spun,
Reflections of grace in the light of the sun.
Each piece a story, each shard a prayer,
Together they sing, in harmony rare.

A journey of healing, through darkness we tread,
With colors of hope, our spirits are fed.
United in spirit, we rise from the fall,
Crafted by hands of the Divine through it all.

Let silence speak volumes where voices have ceased,
In moments of stillness, our hearts find release.
A mosaic of love, intertwined with the real,
In the gallery of faith, the soul learns to heal.

With each chosen heart, a unique design,
Together reflecting the sacred divine.
We are more than mere fragments, together we soar,
A beautiful puzzle, forever explore.

In the sacred assembly, we find our true role,
Every piece matters, the mosaic of soul.
As light fills the gaps, we shine ever bright,
Embracing the journey, we weave through the night.

Gathering Light

In stillness we wait, where shadows abide,
With whispers of hope, let our spirits be tied.
Each flicker a blessing, a divine embrace,
Gathering light in this sacred space.

Through the trials that shape us, we rise and we bend,
In the warmth of connection, our hearts will mend.
A circle of souls, illuminated, we stand,
Lighting the world with a flick of the hand.

With every kind word, like a beacon we shine,
Lifting each other, our souls intertwine.
Gathered in unity, our spirits take flight,
Together we flourish, in the gathering light.

Through valleys of sorrow, we seek out the grace,
In the bonds of compassion, we find our place.
As we walk this journey, our shadows will fade,
For in the gathering light, love's promise is laid.

A melody rises, in harmony sweet,
Voices like thunder, our fears we defeat.
With love at the center, we share and ignite,
A blaze of devotion, in gathering light.

Echoing Faith

In the stillness of prayer, our spirits ascend,
A chorus of echoes, where hearts will blend.
With whispers of hope floating through the night,
Each reverent heartbeat, a source of light.

In valleys of doubt, faith rises anew,
With mountains before us, we press and pursue.
In moments of weakness, we gather our strength,
For faith is the bridge that spans any length.

Through trials and triumphs, our voices unite,
In echoes of kindness, we cherish the light.
A tapestry woven with threads of the true,
Resounding through ages, the promise we knew.

With every creation, a testament stands,
That faith is the compass guiding our hands.
In the silence between us, where love can reside,
We'll echo our faith, forever our guide.

Through seasons of change, our spirits will soar,
In the echoes of faith, we keep seeking more.
With compassion ignited, our hearts intertwined,
Together forever, in love we'll find.

Transitory Gardens

In gardens of time, where moments do bloom,
We tend to the light that dispels the gloom.
With petals of prayer, our spirits will rise,
In transitory spaces, we'll find our skies.

Each season that passes, a lesson to glean,
In the dance of the flowers, a sacred routine.
With roots intertwined, we flourish and grow,
In transitory gardens, our love's gentle glow.

Through shadows and light, we cultivate grace,
In the beauty of change, we find our place.
A garden of hope, with tendrils of faith,
Flourishing freely, in love we embrace.

With hands in the earth, our spirits ignite,
In transitory gardens, we blossom in light.
We walk through the seasons, forever aligned,
With hearts intertwined, and love's harvest designed.

Though petals may fall, their essence remains,
In the cycle of life, resilience sustains.
In transitory gardens, where love's spirit thrives,
We nurture the beauty that forever survives.

Threads of the Ancients

In the stillness of dawn's embrace,
Whispers of the past intertwine,
Echoes of wisdom softly trace,
The divine in every line.

Beneath the sky, the stories unfold,
Of faith that has weathered the storm,
Each thread a bridge, a link of gold,
In the tapestry, we are reborn.

With hands raised high, we seek the light,
Guided by love, not by fear,
Ancients watch us, day and night,
Their teachings woven, ever near.

In silence, we hear the sacred call,
The heartbeat of the universe sings,
In unity, we rise and fall,
For hope and grace are eternal things.

Together we weave, together we stand,
In a circle of life, we learn to grow,
The threads unite as the ancient hand,
Empowers us all, to share and sow.

Merging with the Eternal

In the dance of light, we find our place,
A blending of hearts, a sacred embrace,
In the stillness, souls learn to fly,
Merging with the eternal sky.

Mountains rise, rivers flow,
Time whispers secrets only few know,
In the sacred space of the now,
We dive into the divine somehow.

Voices of ages call out to me,
Guiding my path, setting me free,
With each breath, I feel the grace,
As I merge with the vastness of space.

Through trials and tears, we seek the light,
In unity's arms, taking flight,
With each moment, we grow and thrive,
In the essence of love, we truly arrive.

As the stars align, destiny flows,
Together in faith, compassion grows,
In this journey, hand in hand,
We merge with the eternal, ever grand.

Blossoms of Wisdom

In the garden where spirits bloom,
The petals of truth dispel the gloom,
Each blossom a lesson, vibrant and bright,
A beacon of love, guiding our sight.

Roots intertwined, wisdom of old,
Grounded in faith, our stories unfold,
From soil of sorrow, to the light of day,
In every struggle, wisdom finds its way.

Beneath the sun, we gather each morn,
To cherish the gifts of the souls reborn,
For every heart that beats in the now,
Holds blossoms of wisdom, this sacred vow.

With gentle hands, we tend the ground,
Nurturing dreams where love is found,
In every season, together we grow,
The blossoms of wisdom, a radiant show.

So let us marvel at nature's grace,
In unity, we find our place,
And in the garden of life, we prepare,
To gather the fruits, and tenderly share.

The Covenant of Years

In the embrace of time, we stand,
A covenant bound by love's gentle hand,
Each year a chapter, rich and profound,
In the circle of life, we gather around.

With every heartbeat, stories ignite,
Threads of the past merge with the light,
In the fabric of days, hope is spun,
An eternal dance, we are never undone.

As seasons change, we learn and grow,
In the whispers of ages, the truth we sow,
With gratitude, we honor our fears,
In the embrace of the covenant of years.

Together we walk, hand in hand,
Through valleys of shadow, on faith we stand,
In unity, we rise, in love we remain,
The covenant of years, a sacred refrain.

At twilight's edge, we shall reflect,
On the blessings of time and what we collect,
In this bond, may we always see,
The beauty of life and its mystery.

The Crucible of Life

In trials we stand, hearts bold and true,
The fire refines all that we pursue.
Faith like gold, through heat it shines,
In the crucible of life, the spirit aligns.

Each burden we bear, a step to grace,
In shadows we wander, yet seek His face.
Through suffering's path, our souls awake,
In every challenge, love we partake.

The mountains may rise, yet we will climb,
With every heartbeat, we cherish time.
In the furnace of hope, we are reborn,
A testament to strength, where dreams are worn.

From ashes we gather, to forge our way,
In faith's embrace, we find our stay.
The Crucible of Life, a sacred trial,
In every tear, there's beauty to compile.

So let us rejoice, in shadows or light,
With hearts ignited, we take our flight.
For in every moment, His love we see,
A journey of purpose, eternally free.

Moments of Divine Alignment

In silence we gather, souls intertwined,
The whispers of heaven are gently aligned.
Each heartbeat a rhythm, a sacred sign,
Moments unfold, in a dance so divine.

Through the chaos of days, we seek the truth,
In laughter and tears, we nurture our youth.
Threads of the cosmos, woven so tight,
Illuminate paths through the shadows of night.

When time seems to pause, we breathe in grace,
Instants of light in a vast, sacred space.
With faith as our compass, we navigate fate,
Moments of love that we cultivate.

As stars shimmer brightly, guiding our way,
Each moment a blessing, come what may.
In unity's strength, we rise and entwine,
Living the echoes of moments divine.

So cherish each breath, for it's a gift,
In the tapestry of life, let our spirits lift.
For in every encounter, we see Him revealed,
Moments of alignment, our hearts are healed.

Rising from Ashes

From the depths of despair, we find our flight,
Ashes transform into wings of light.
With every setback, a lesson learned,
In the furnace of trials, our passions burned.

Through shadows of doubt, we walk with grace,
Each fall a reminder to embrace our place.
For in every wound, a story is spun,
Rising from ashes, our journey's begun.

The phoenix within, ignited by fire,
Fueled by love's flame, we rise ever higher.
With hearts open wide, we greet the dawn,
In the beauty of struggle, we are reborn.

With courage our cloak, we face the storm,
Transforming our pain into something warm.
Rising from ashes, we spread our wings,
In the symphony of life, our spirit sings.

So let the world watch as we take our stand,
Crafting our dreams with a steady hand.
For in every end, there's a glorious start,
Rising from ashes, we follow our heart.

The Inner Sanctuary

In the stillness of soul, we find our home,
A place of refuge, where the spirit roams.
In whispers of prayer, we feel his light,
The Inner Sanctuary, pure and bright.

With faith as our anchor, we shield our hearts,
In silence we gather, as wisdom imparts.
Each moment a blessing, each breath divine,
Within this sacred space, our souls align.

The chaos outside may swirl and churn,
Yet in this haven, our spirits learn.
With every heartbeat, we connect the dots,
In the Inner Sanctuary, fear is forgot.

Through trials we face, this peace abides,
A garden of grace where hope resides.
In the depths of the storm, we see the truth,
The Inner Sanctuary, eternal youth.

So gather your thoughts, let your spirit soar,
In the quiet of love, we find the door.
For in every heartbeat, in every sigh,
The Inner Sanctuary calls us to fly.

Resonance of the Ages

In silence deep, the echoes sing,
Of faith and hope, our souls take wing.
Through trials faced, we find the light,
And grasp the truth, dispelling night.

The wisdom passed from sage to sage,
Awakens hearts, transcends the age.
In every prayer, a promise made,
In every tear, the light shall braid.

The stars above, in skies so wide,
Remind us all of the divine guide.
As rivers flow, the spirit moves,
Each rhythm shared, our faith approves.

In community, our voices rise,
A chorus bright that fills the skies.
With love we weave the sacred thread,
A tapestry where hope is fed.

So let us walk this ancient way,
In service true, both night and day.
For in our hearts, the truth remains,
Resonance felt, eternal gains.

Cultivating Forth

In fields of grace, new seeds are sown,
With tender hands, in love we've grown.
Through seasons change, we learn to trust,
That faith will bloom from humble dust.

The sun breaks forth with radiant beams,
Awakening all our deepest dreams.
With every prayer, our roots go deep,
In quiet moments, our spirit we keep.

Through doubt and fear, we journey on,
With kindred hearts, we face the dawn.
In every challenge, a lesson learned,
In every sacrifice, our passion burned.

With grateful hearts, we gather near,
In gratitude, we cast out fear.
For every tear, a blessing flows,
In every heart, the garden grows.

So cultivate, with love and grace,
The sacred ground, a holy place.
In unity, our spirits rise,
To reach the heavens, touch the skies.

Sacred Journey of the Heart

Upon this path, our spirits tread,
With open hearts, by love we're led.
In every step, the light will reign,
Signposts of hope, amid the pain.

The whispers soft, of ancient lore,
Guide weary souls, to seek for more.
In silence found, the truth reveals,
A sacred journey, the heart heals.

Through trials faced, compassion blooms,
In darkened times, the light consumes.
Each tear we shed, a prayer ascends,
In bonds of grace, all sorrow mends.

So let us walk, hand in hand,
On this path, together stand.
With every heartbeat, love will chart,
The sacred journey of the heart.

In each embrace, the spirit grows,
In every kindness, our essence glows.
From depths of soul, let love impart,
The sacred journey, a work of art.

The Unseen Hand

In quiet moments, shadows blend,
A guiding force, our faithful friend.
Though eyes may close, the heart can see,
The unseen hand that sets us free.

With gentle grace, it leads us on,
Through valleys deep, beneath the dawn.
In every twist, a mystic thread,
The patterns weave where spirit's led.

Through pain and loss, the path is drawn,
A tapestry, where hope's reborn.
In every struggle, a lesson stays,
In every moment, our spirit plays.

The universe, in whispers bold,
Conveys the truth in tales retold.
With every heartbeat, we respond,
To the unseen hand, so very fond.

So trust the journey, for we are near,
In every breath, the love is clear.
With faith unfurled, let us withstand,
The gentle touch of the unseen hand.

Milton Keynes UK
Ingram Content Group UK Ltd.
UKHW022118251124
451529UK00012B/599